Fabulous

Fabulous

Anne Pollard

Fabulous

Copyright © 2024 by Anne Pollard. All rights reserved.

No part of this publication may be reproduced, distributed, or transmitted in any form or by any means, including photocopying, recording, or other electronic or mechanical methods, without the prior written permission of the author, except in the case of brief quotations embodied in critical reviews and certain other noncommercial uses permitted by copyright law.

The contents of this work, including, but not limited to, the accuracy of events, people, and places depicted; opinions expressed; permission to use previously published materials included; and any advice given or actions advocated are solely the responsibility of the author, who assumes all liability for said work and indemnifies the publisher against any claims stemming from publication of the work.

Printed in the United States of America
ISBN 978-1-64133-912-4 (sc)
ISBN 978-1-64133-913-1 (e)
ISBN 978-1-64133-911-7 (hc)

2024.07.15

This book is printed on acid-free paper.

Because of the dynamic nature of the Internet, any web addresses or links contained in this book may have changed since publication and may no longer be valid. The views expressed in this work are solely those of the author and do not necessarily reflect the views of the publisher, and the publisher hereby disclaims any responsibility for them.

Blue Ink Media Solutions
1111B S Governors Ave
STE 7582 Dover,
DE 19904

www.blueinkmediasolutions.com

Foreword

One of my dear friends says that everyone has a word. A word that they use all of the time and mostly are unaware of it. I think that's right. She told me my word is FABULOUS. And although my entire life is not necessarily what I would have called fabulous, the life I choose now is so much more than that. And the crazy thing is that your life can be just as "beyond fabulous" as mine! And it's so easy.

But I am getting ahead of myself.

This book is my way of sharing the path that I took over the last decade to become so happy. To see the magic and miracles that happen every hour of every day. To invite you to see them as well and live a life that is truly rainbows and unicorns (they do exist you know).

So, when you are ready to choose:

- *happiness instead of sadness*
- *love instead of hate*
- *compassion instead of anger*

FABULOUS

- *self-love instead of jealousy*
- *peace instead of anxiety*

then call me and let's go play among the stars.

Looking Back

If you have never looked back at your life from where you are today, I encourage you to do so. It's quite an eye-opener when you are on your journey of life. As I look back over my life, mostly the past decade, I can trace my present joy back to what has happened over the years and I can clearly see how each event brought me to the person I am now. I no longer believe in living in the past or the future but it was an amazing eye-opener when I reviewed the past ten years and was able to see the gifts that The Universe so lovingly gave me.

My past decade was full of life and what life brings to all of us. I went through loss, solitude, happiness, revitalization, retirement and transformation. Through all of those gifts from The Universe, I have had my eyes opened to so many things. I want to share with you some of those fabulous things as an inspiration so that perhaps you can find your own insights, life purpose and inner peace, but also to know who you really are inside. I am completely convinced that we are all here to play, have fun, love, laugh and live each day to our highest purpose. And to help move the world to a better place, support our fellow humans and drink in the beauty of the earth in all of its splendor. The Universe is such a giving place and to connect to all of that goodness, you only need to ask. There is so much support out there for us and it is only full of love. And we can all connect to those wonderful things just by asking to make it so. Then have some gratitude for everything that life sends your way, because regardless of whether we label life's events as good or bad, they are all opportunities to learn and grow.

My Transformation Trifecta

We have all been through great loss, some more than others I suppose. My great losses started in 2012 when my marriage of 22 years suddenly came to an abrupt end. Overnight, my marriage was over. When something like that happens to you, your whole world caves in and you feel like you can't breathe, you can't move and you can't see how you will get through the next minute, hour or day. At least, that's how I felt. And I know most of you have had a similar experience whether it was your spouse, someone in your family or perhaps a friend. It's the kind of pain that cuts you to your very core and one you feel like you will never get past. For me, getting through the pain and now reflecting on that time, it was really about the **animals**, the **friends** and the **music**.

The Animals. I was blessed at the time with two of the most loving and innocent souls to support and guide me through that difficult time in my life, Willa and Maggie. They were my two Bernese Mountain Dogs and they saved my life. Did you know that in the world of animal spirits, the dog spirit represents healing emotional wounds, unconditional love, loyalty and protection? Their spirit and their love are ever-present and on the worst days, they can make you laugh and play, even if just for a moment. Willa and Maggie did so much more than that. On the really bad days, they made me go outside and smell the fresh air, run and play frisbee and laugh at their crazy antics.

The Friends. True friends are the other best therapy for what ails you. And when I say *true* friends, they are a different sort than the friends that you meet occasionally for drinks and dinner. True friends are the ones that really listen when you need to vent, they never judge you and you always feel better when you are with them. I am blessed to have several true friends who were there to support me during those dark years. Always checking in with me and making sure I could get through one more day. Sometimes they would just pop in my office and sit for a minute and send healing, loving vibes my way. Friends are the spice and icing in your life and to have a true friend, you must first *be* a true friend. Because what is inside you reflects out and attracts more of what it is, back to you. So, if you are true friend to someone else, that attraction magnifies and draws true friends back to you.

The Music. The trifecta of the healing and transforming formula. Music is a gift that knows no rival. There is something for everyone and it's a very personal thing when you find artists and songs that speak to you. I also believe it is how The Universe speaks to me. We all have an inner wavelength that is connected to a higher vibration and music is the energy that connects it all together. Think about how you feel when your favorite song comes on. You can't help at least tapping your foot or humming along. For me, music is a reflection of my mood and I can use it to change my mood at any moment. It is one of the most important things in my life. During the dark years, music helped me cry, helped me grieve, and helped me finally start healing and living again.

The Solitude Years

I am an Aquarian through and through. If you look up Aquarius in the astrological signs, you will find me. And boy do I believe in astrology! I am a dreamer, a deep thinker and always a little on the outskirts of normal society. I believe in all things, whether of this world or others, and I am always open to new concepts and ideas. I have a vision of what I think is right and just. It is my internal set of scales in which giving and receiving have to be in balance. I am intuitive, creative, and I care a lot about the state of the world and how to make things better. I love to talk and engage in long conversations, sometimes about really deep subjects, but I am less prone to just ordinary small talk. Mental connections are very important to me and are the basis for all of my close relationships. I am a free spirit and extremely independent. I plan for and relish my time to myself, because I need a lot of it. I get highly engaged in projects and relationships and then sometimes get bored with them after a short while and move on to something else. I am not drawn to a parent-child relationship and thus never wanted or planned to have children of my own, which I do not. I may not always come across as

The Solitude Years

warm and compassionate, but I have a soft side that is always present and no one is a truer friend. I love being charitable and I cannot ever say no to someone in need. I love seeing the beauty in the world and I am most at home and at peace in nature.

So why am I telling you about me as an Aquarian? I do that because I think it is important for you to have some context about the type of person I am so you can relate that to my story. Your story may look very different from mine, even with the exact same events, because each of us sees the world through our own lens. I hope you now have a better understanding of what my lens looks like. It's important, because what I share with you about my road to happiness may not resemble your road at all. And that's the point. You have to find your *thing*, what brings you more joy than anything else to get to the place I am now. And you all have it; you just may not know it yet.

After the initial shock of me being on my own had mostly subsided, I entered into what I call the solitude years. It would be about 8 years and would be filled with gifts of sorrow, love, abundance, utter sadness and soul searching.

I was completely convinced that I no longer wanted a man in my life and I shut off my heart to that type of love. I was extremely busy with work and the long hours and travel occupied me for the most part. If I wasn't working, I was with Willa and Maggie at home, playing frisbee with them and working in the yard, tending to the grass and the flowers and always coming up with a new landscaping project to occupy my time. I rarely went out to meet family or friends, because I always felt so guilty about not spending enough time with the dogs. And like I said, I love my time alone and I got plenty of it during those years.

I was blessed with being able to work with some amazing people in amazing places all around the world. It was especially difficult leaving Willa and Maggie when I traveled because they were not well-adapted to staying in a kennel or dog park of any kind. I wanted them to be able to stay at the house, hoping that would be less stressful for them when I was gone. I know that anyone who has a dog understands the pain and guilt you feel when you look at their faces as you pack your suitcase. Most of my trips were international so I would be gone for a week or more each time I left. I needed someone that I trusted to stay at the house with the girls when I was gone. That's when I met my best friend. She was introduced to me through another friend and she was willing to come and take care of Willa and Maggie while I was gone. Remember when I was talking about events, people, animals and music and how all of that wove through my life? Here we are again. The events of traveling to Europe, the Middle East and South America were a fabulous way to spend time without thinking about how depressed I was most days. Willa and Maggie were still the center of my life and most of the joy in my life. The music selection was changing as I relived my past from the 70's and 80's through various rock and roll bands, re-discovering artists from my past and enjoying some loud crazy tunes. I went from really sad and heartfelt songs to a more upbeat playlist. But I still used music as my anchor and joy when I was traveling or working in the yard. I wouldn't say I was happy, but I was feeling better each day as the pain continued to subside. Since I relish my time alone, the lack of a man in my life was not really a problem and I am not someone who needs to be in a relationship all of the time, so turning that part of my life completely off wasn't really that difficult. What took the place of that need for closeness were my true friends. I worked with several people who became, and still are, the joy of my life. I liked going into the office and spending time with them. I mentored people in the office and was the office sounding-board when people needed to vent, ask for advice or just step away from the rat race for a few minutes to have some M&M's and share a smile. That was the joy in my life and probably why I worked so many hours. I was always overjoyed though to come home to Willa and Maggie. There is no better feeling I think in the world than walking in the door and being greeted by the most loving, playful and hungry dogs!

Of course, various things happened during those years, some good things and some bad things. At least that's how I would refer to those events at that time. Even though Maggie was younger than Willa, she developed liver cancer and died in 2016 at the age of seven. I don't think I can recall a worse day in my entire life. I won't elaborate on the details, but suffice it to say that it was unexpected and I have never felt the level of total loss and devastation as I did that day. It rocked my world to the very core. I spent endless days and nights crying my eyes out and had it not been for Willa still at my side, I'm not sure I would have made it through those months of complete anguish. But The Universe always sends you angels and again, my true friends were there one hundred percent. My best friend was there for me all of the time and made sure I knew that I was loved and that Maggie was missed. The music switched back to soulful, depressing songs. I grieved for Maggie through the music for a long time. I also spent a lot of time on the patio in the back yard. That's when the deer began to come. The Universe sends angels in all sorts of forms and the deer that came into my world were my new angels. Willa and I would sit on the patio and watch them amble across the back yard woods and Willa would not even get up to chase them. They became very important to my connection with The Universe and nature and continue to be so even through today.

It would only be one year later when Willa passed to the Rainbow Bridge. She died of old age in 2017 and her passing was more natural than Maggie's, but the pain was just as real and just as devastating. The two most important things in my life were gone and at times, I felt like the grief was unbearable. I wanted to just lay down and die so many times during that time. I could not let go of them and I sought solace through reading about how to connect to your pets once they passed. Since I believe in all things of this world and beyond, I believed that if I could connect with them in their afterlife, I would

The Solitude Years

find some kind of peace. As it turned out, that didn't happen for about 5 years. But I watched for signs from them all the time and I found feathers and pennies on a regular basis which are signs that an angel is watching over you. And it was always a comfort. I still have all of the feathers and pennies that they have sent through the years and I still find solace in them, although now in a different way.

Abundance

I'll take a short step back now and talk about abundance. It is one of my favorite words and is a feeling and state of mind that I have had for many years. Many years ago, I was introduced to *The Secret*, by Rhonda Byrne. If you have never read the book or seen the video, I encourage you to do so. Seeing that video planted a seed in me that ultimately grew into a lifelong absolute. **Abundance**. I immersed myself in books and would listen to tapes about abundance when I was in the car. I am a voracious reader and it is one of my favorite pass times. I read every book I could find about getting rich, loving money and being wealthy. It's funny, I had forgotten about all of that until I wrote this book. The daily actions faded over time but the seed was planted forever and it continued to blossom through my life. I have always been blessed with great jobs and had a fabulous career through the years. Through a lot of dedication and hard work, I had a good income that became a great income. I'm not talking fabulously wealthy, but I certainly made enough to live comfortably. But I had to get past a lot of debt! The debt from my marriage that I had to carry on my own was almost staggering. My friends even suggested that I declare bankruptcy to get out from underneath it. But the Aquarian in me could not walk away from my previous financial actions and decisions and to walk away from that debt, when it was my decision to spend that money, felt wrong in every possible way. So instead, I told myself that I would pay it all off, a little at a time, until I was whole again. It's funny how embarrassed I was to even tell people how much debt I was in and thus I only told a very few people. Suffice it to say, it was six digits. But I always held the firm belief in my heart and soul that I could get beyond it and get back to a place of prosperity. Abundance. It took years and years and a lot of financial planning to get there but I never lacked for things I needed and I had a firm plan to pay off the debt, which I did. Sometimes I didn't know how it would happen, and I have come to learn that I didn't need to know how. Just know it will happen. Be in the flow. Money is energy and it has to flow in and out.

There were some really fabulous days during those years when each credit card or each loan was closed. I remember so distinctly the day I went to the bank to pay off the second mortgage. The bank tellers were so professional when I walked up to the counter to give them the certified check to pay off the account but by the end of the transaction, we were high-fiving and laughing about men, divorce, debt and coming out on the other side as a better and stronger person. But as I started believing then, abundance is a choice that you make. You make that choice in your heart, your head, your words and your actions. For example, I have always had a hard time using coupons, because to me, coupons signified that I didn't have enough to buy something at full price. It wasn't the few dollars that I would save, it was more the mindset that I needed them to get what I wanted. Now that is not to say anything negative about people who use coupons and please don't take it that way. Again, that was my lens and my lens only. It may not be yours nor does it need to be. The point is more that you believe and act as if you have abundance and it will come to you, exponentially. Over the years, I have given money to several people who were really in need, with no expectation to get that money back. Some would say significant amounts of money. But the rule of abundance is that you give from the heart and everything you give will come back to you. I really believe that is true and I have proven it in my life over and over again. It makes me a little sad to hear how most people talk about money and wealth. As I listen, most people I know talk about not having enough money or that thing is too expensive and I can't afford it. My firm belief is that if you say you can't afford it, especially when you say it out loud, then you will never be able to afford it. What you say is so very important. The Universe is always listening and trying to fulfil your dreams, and The Universe will always give you more of what you are speaking, thinking and visualizing. So, when you say out loud that you are poor or you can't afford it or can't … (fill in the blank) then The Universe will give that to you because that is where your thoughts and words are. That is what you are sending out to the world and that is what you will attract back to you. If I could eliminate one word from the human language, it would be **can't**. It is the most destructive word that I know. It only takes being aware of your words and just even slightly changing what you say to remove that awful word, can't, and your life will change a thousand ways.

I don't believe that money is evil or bad or having money will make you a bad person. Sure, there are those that exploit and do bad things for money, but that doesn't mean it's that way for everyone. I believe that The Universe wants us to be happy and abundant and to use our resources to make this world a better place. Money is one part of an abundant life and it's not a bad part. Abundance is a state of mind and it is our birthright. How can you be happy and at peace if you think you can't pay your bills or help a friend or make the world a better place to live? We put ourselves on this earth to play and have fun and help others and money is a part of that equation. And it's a large part of my transformation. But more about that later on.

So why did I take a step back to talk about Abundance? Well, it was such a large part of the next phase of my transformation, the Awakening Years.

The Awakening Years

A fter the eight years of solitude, I moved into what I call the Awakening Years. That really started about 2016.

Going away to college was one of the best experiences of my life. During freshman year, I met a group of girls that I connected with so much that they are still all in my life today (40 years later) and we always have so much fun together. We are the group that when we get together, it is like we have never been apart. We are all so different in so many ways but so alike in other ways. We always stayed in touch after graduation, some years more than others, and we attended each other's weddings through the years as well. Later on, we started doing reunions every few years to see each other and spend some fun time in various places in the US. We are all over the US now from the East Coast to the West Coast and points in between and we varied our trips accordingly. In 2016 we met at the beach for our reunion. I was so thrilled to see them again! We rented a house on the water and spent time catching up with what was happening in each other's lives. They all had children and all were still married and the conversations mostly migrated to the husbands and the children. Through the weekend, I began to get more and more depressed hearing about their lives and wondering why I was the only one in the group that had divorced. And each time the conversation shifted to the children, I withdrew further and further. During that weekend, I felt so alone and I secretly resented them for their great lives and looked back at mine wondering where I had gone wrong. It got so bad that I ended up leaving early. Of course, they never knew how I felt that weekend and I'm not sure why I didn't tell them, since we talk about everything, but I guess that's just where I was in my journey at the time. But I could always go home to Willa and Maggie and the pain would subside or I could push it away or push it deeper.

Maggie

Maggie

Maggie was the younger of my two Bernese Mountain dogs and when we decided that Willa needed a friend, we found Maggie. She was really young when we got her, so we imprinted with Maggie at a very young age. Willa took to her almost immediately and I think she looked to Willa as her mom. They were so cute together as Maggie grew up. As we all bonded, I felt a very close relationship to Maggie. Her energy was so aligned with mine. She had the greatest smile that a dog can have and she always made me laugh. When she was young, we would encourage her to get a toy when she got excited or when we came home and that became imprinted in her forever. She was rarely seen without some kind of stuffed toy in her mouth and many times she would grab two or three toys at the same time! It would make you laugh so hard to see her running through the house with a mouthful of toys that she could barely even hold.

Maggie was also my helper outside. When it was too hot for Willa to stay outside while I was doing yard work or projects, Maggie was ALWAYS there by my side. When I raked leaves, she would hang in the yard until she couldn't stand it any longer and she would grab her frisbee and trot over to me for a little fun and games. And she always knew I would stop and play. We had so much joy! If I was trimming bushes, she would come and lay right in the middle of the brush pile. When I was doing a stone pathway in the backyard, she would come and lay right where I was going to lay the next stone. If I was planting a new bush, she would be right beside the hole I just dug. And always smiling and always so full of love and contentment.

She was also my dinner companion most evenings and would always be grateful for a little bite of whatever I was having. Willa always maintained a nonchalant distance but Maggie was right there at my feet, looking up at me with those big eyes, and acting as if she hadn't eaten in weeks.

Mags was the funny, smiley one. My friend said that Willa was the queen and Maggie was the jester. She was so right! Maggie was such pure innocence and love and it shined out of her through her eyes, her smile and her very essence. There was no way you could be in a bad mood when Mags came running around the corner with the toy of the day hanging out of her mouth. And even as she had a mouth full of fuzzy ball or toy squirrel or sometimes both, her smile was so big and beautiful that you were instantly compelled to smile back. But the frisbee was her all-time favorite. She couldn't leave the house to play unless she had a frisbee in her mouth and a smile on her face. We would spend hours in the back yard, running, throwing frisbee, rolling in the leaves and just being.

And Maggie loved for me to sing to her! Those were the years of Bon Jovi and Phil Collins. I still have such a strong connection to her through that music, especially Phil Collins. My favorite Phil Collins song to sing to her was "Two Hearts", and I felt that with her in every cell of my body. I would sing and look at her and her smile was a mile long. There was literally no way I could be unhappy when I was with Maggie. She was my soulmate, my angel, my muse and my constant companion.

And then she got sick. I didn't know what was wrong with her when her eating dropped off and she began to lose a lot of weight. Many trips to the vet did not turn up anything right away. I was still traveling at the time and I was so worried about her each time I left. It got so bad that I took her to the emergency vet clinic the weekend I returned from a trip and they diagnosed her with liver cancer. The vet offered that we could do chemotherapy and that it would extend her life by a little time, but I could not put her through that kind of pain and suffering. She had had enough. Mags passed to Rainbow Bridge on October 10, 2016. As I said previously, it was the worst day of my life. But my true friends were there for me 100%. My best friend immediately brought me a plant and left it at the door since I could not face seeing anyone at that time. I texted another of my close friends that she had passed and he came over with flowers and a card even though he had just gotten back from vacation that same day. True friends. They are always there for you in the best and the worst of times.

My music selection changed to the most sad, soulful songs I could find. I made a playlist of the most beautiful and sorrowful songs, mostly again from Phil Collins. He can really touch your soul with his music. If you have never heard "Undertow", that one will really wrench your heart out. I was in the worst place I have ever been in my life and every day I would sit outside in the evening and just cry my eyes out. Again, if not for Willa, I probably would have just laid down and died. It was the closest I have ever come to really thinking about suicide and I did think about it often. There was nothing that could soothe my grief and I was in mourning for years. I began to look up all of the videos on YouTube about pets passing and how to communicate with them. I needed to speak to her, to connect with her, to ease my pain in any way I could find. Nothing really helped but I kept looking for solace in videos, pet whispers and songs. It wasn't until 2022 when I finally came to peace about her and Willa.

After Mags passed, I was extremely dependent on Willa for love and companionship and she did not disappoint. Willa was my rock. She was a very silent sufferer and I know that she missed Maggie as much as I did. But we kept each other together as best we could through the next six months.

Willa

FABULOUS

Willa was a very typical Bernese Mountain dog, with the looks and temperament of one of the greatest dog breeds there is. She was everything a Berner should be and she sure did love the cold. One thing about Willa, she would pant even if she was laying in the snow. She had the most beautiful eyes and was very attune to the world around her. Perhaps even psychic. When we got Willa as a puppy, we also had two border collies. Shelly was aging and we knew would not live too much longer. Duncan was a rescue dog and always had problems with shyness and the desire to be alone. He was suffering from something we could not diagnose or identify and it was not something physiological, so we got the name of a pet whisperer from a friend and called her to come do a reading on Duncan. She was quite an amazing person and when she came over to the house, we asked her to tell us what she was feeling and seeing about Duncan. Before she would do that, she asked about Willa and commented that she was getting really strong vibes from Willa and that Willa was quite conscious and aware of things that were perhaps even hidden from us. This was later revealed to be 100% true. You see, Duncan had a lot of internal immunity issues but hid them for a long time. However, Willa knew that, and she began to try and protect Duncan from other people and other dogs when we took them out for walks. We didn't notice what the behavior was at the time and unfortunately it took its toll on Willa. She became extremely shy from all strangers and only trusted a very few people. Her personality changed completely. It got to the point that we could not even get her out of the car to go anywhere, especially to the vet. We would have to pick her up out of the car and carry her inside the vet's office. And you can imagine that is not an easy thing to do with a Bernese Mountain Dog. They are huge!

We did put Willa into immersive training and it helped enough that she could live a relatively normal life. But she and Maggie were tight right from the start. Willa taught Maggie how to use the doggie door, where to play in the yard and find the rabbit poop (why do dogs love rabbit poop so much!!!!) and just in general how to play and have fun. Maggie would follow Willa around, eat next to her, lay down beside her and they would hang together outside for hours. She was the best "mom" dog anyone could have. And even though a lot of Willa's life was spent in internal fear and anxiety, when it was just the three of us, she was the strongest, most loving being you could ever know.

Willa was a hugger. I would be standing in the yard after a round of frisbee, and she would run full-speed down the hill, amazingly stop short right in front of me and then she would stand on her back legs, reach up and hug me. It makes me laugh and smile even now just thinking about it. **I am a hugger** and she knew that so well. Every time she hugged me, I smiled and laughed and hugged her back. What a fabulous thing to feel from an animal that knows you probably better than you know yourself. And every time she hugged me, my emotional wounds eased, just a bit.

As I said, Willa was older than Maggie and as those of you who have owned large-breed dogs know, the sad part is that they do not live very long. The average life for a Berner is about 6 - 8 years. So, anything longer than that is a daily blessing. And I was blessed to have her for 11 years. I told you; she was a rock. After Maggie passed, Willa began to really start showing her signs of aging. She had trouble getting up off the hard wood floors so I had rugs everywhere in the house to help her with her grip. I live in a two-story house and the bedrooms are upstairs. But like the champ she was, she would climb those stairs every night to go to bed. Some nights she had to really work up the courage to do that and would stand at the bottom of the stairs for 5 - 10 minutes before she could muster the strength to make it up that first step. I would help her of course but I could not carry her.

Willa passed to the Rainbow Bridge on July 21, 2017.

I am one hundred percent sure that The Universe sent Willa and Maggie to me as my guardian angels, to watch over me and love me and just be with me during my years of solitude. Both of them are still with me every day, their spirit shines on me always. It would not be until my awakening that I was able to release all of the grief and understand that they are truly always around me and really never left me, even though they left their physical bodies.

Working Through the Pain

As I struggled to get through each day once my fur babies were gone, my work became the main focus of my time. The travel was picking up and I was gone quite a lot. But I still watched dog videos of Willa and Mags every night on my tablet before I went to sleep. Most nights, I cried myself to sleep. It was my own private Hell. I pushed the pain deeper and deeper and never showed anyone that side of me. I felt that I had to act like the senior director that I was and so I moved through the year working long hours and doing my best to support my team and co-workers, ignoring the pain I crawled inside every day.

I did lots of house projects that next year, like remodeling the kitchen and the basement. It was a good distraction and it does make you feel better when you can see the results of that kind of renovation. And truth be told, it was much easier to do that kind of work in the house without having to worry about the dogs.

In 2017, I flew so much that it was the equivalent of flying around the world. In 2018, that ramped up even more. I flew the equivalent of two and a half times around the world. Though mostly trips to Europe, I also had the fabulous opportunity to visit some amazing places like Czech Republic, Sweden, Morocco, Spain, Oman, Dubai and Mexico. And even though I was American, I was greeted by the most gracious people you will ever find. I love to travel and meet new people and visit new places and this was the whirlwind opportunity to do just that.

One day, when I went out to get the mail, I was surprised to find a letter from the airlines that I flew most frequently congratulating me on becoming a member of their concierge key program. I didn't really know much about it, other than when I was standing in line waiting to board, they always called this group of people to board first in front of everyone else! To this day, I don't know how or why I was selected, but it has been the most fabulous part of my travel life. I hear a lot of people say that customer service is a dying art these days, but then, I guess they don't know about this amazing group. I think these folks wrote the book on how to treat a customer in every facet of their interactions. They greet you at the airport, make sure you have everything you need, print your boarding pass, escort you on and off the plane and make sure you get wherever you need to be, all with the most gracious smiles. I was traveling home from Europe and had to connect through London most of the time. If you have been through any London airport, then you know what an absolute pain it is to transfer terminals on the airport buses and trains, go through security and get to your connection in under an hour. On this particular trip, my first flight out was delayed. We were so late leaving that I knew I would never make the connection in London. I called the airline special support staff to try and get booked on the later flight out of London. When I explained the delay, the agent assured me that they could get me through the airport in time to make my connection. I nervously thought about how they would make that happen the whole way to London. One of the greatest perks of being in this status is that they transport you from terminal to terminal in a limo instead of the buses and trains. So, when I arrived in London and departed the plane, I was greeted by an agent who whisked me away in a limo to the connecting terminal, all the while ensuring me that I would make the flight. We arrived at the departing terminal where she walked me to the front of the security line, politely asking the agent to please squeeze me in next, which he did. After getting through security, the agent then walked with me to the airline lounge where they checked my flight and seat assignment to ensure everything was correct and I even had time to have a drink! She then walked me to the gate, escorted me to the front of the line and made sure that I boarded safely and with time to spare. Whew!

Now, I'm telling you this story to illustrate what real service to others looks like and how it makes you feel when someone is dedicated to making you happy. This wonderful person did everything she could to ensure that I was happy and made my connection. And since

I am telling you this story five years after it happened, it clearly had a huge impact on me. I not only distinctly remember that entire day and how grateful it made me feel, it reminded me and inspired me that doing something for someone else, no matter how big or small, can make a lasting impression on them in a positive way. And shouldn't that be why we are all here? When you do one positive thing, especially when you do it with love in your heart, you can change the world, one person at a time. If you don't believe me, try it. Make it a point to do something unexpectedly nice for someone else for no reason other than it feels good. Don't have any expectation for reward or thanks and maybe even do it anonymously! See if it gives you joy and a feeling that will keep you smiling for days. And it will also inspire others to do the same. Pay it forward, because it really does make a difference.

What? Motorcycles?

Around 2018, a close friend reached out one day to see if I would like to ride motorcycles with them. They have ridden motorcycles for a large part of their adult life and it is something they enjoy tremendously. I had free time and no dogs to hold me at home, so on a whim, I agreed to go for a ride. I rode on the back of the bike with one of my friends while my other friend rode her own. I have to admit I was really scared to take that first ride, but as I relaxed and got in the flow of the motion of the bike, something clicked in me that this was the most fabulous feeling in the world! And I would definitely have to do this again. Which I did, from then on, as often as I could.

FABULOUS

Riding motorcycles awakened a part of me that I now embrace with passion. As an Aquarian, I have a side of me that is a wild, free spirit and riding gave me the outlet to be who I really wanted to be, and who I could not be when I was working in the corporate world. It is the most amazing feeling to be in the wind, smell the farms along the road, feel the sun on your face and shoulders, and hear the sounds of the world, just enjoy being alive. The bikers call it "wind therapy" and boy are they right! If you have any doubts, check out the number of motorcycles in front of a psychiatrist office.... you won't find any! It is one of the greatest ways to connect to your inner soul that I have ever found. You've heard of walking meditation but riding meditation is even better. And oh, can I talk about the bling! I love shiny, sparkly things and always have. The motorcycle world puts a whole new dimension to bling! You should see my riding wardrobe. It rocks! You can become a completely different person through the leather chaps and jackets, and let me just say that I have found the real me! I am now fully-entrenched in the lifestyle and would not trade a moment of that part of my life, then or now.

The Second College Reunion

In July of 2018, the college girls were itching for a reunion so we decided to invade the vacation home of our friend who lives out west. We all met at the airport coming in from all over the country. It was such a great time to see the life-long friends again and enjoy another great weekend away. We got our cars and headed to the house. I think all of our jaws dropped open when we saw this gorgeous "log cabin"! It was breath-taking – the house, the view, everything was so beautiful. It is nice to have friends who have done well for themselves.

We enjoyed the time to catch up, do some shopping, just hanging out and being our real selves again for a while. I will admit that I was on my guard a bit from the last reunion but their kids were growing up and the conversation was less about that and more about us. We cooked dinner one night and were sitting around afterwards having some wine and good conversation when the topic turned to me and my "singleness". I am still the only one in the group that is divorced and have no children so I guess I will always remain the exception to the rule. We started talking about me and being single and my interpretation of the conversation was that I should find a man. Their feeling was that life is better with a partner and that really set me off! I tried to explain that I was happy with where I was and that I didn't need a man to complete me in any way. The conversation got heated and for sure, I over-reacted. At the time, I was truly OK with being single and I loved my time to myself and shouldn't that be enough? Remember that lens thing that I was talking about? My lens said it was absolutely OK to be on your own, while their lens said I could be happier. As I look back on that conversation now, I can see that they only wanted me to be happy and that was what they thought happy was, from their lens. I didn't agree at the time and I still vehemently think that if someone chooses to be single, that's absolutely what they should be. We of course got past it, as all friends ultimately do, but it left a little voice in my head as we departed. I believe that you have to be happy with you and you only before you can invite another into your life. I still had some work to do before I was there.

The Career Takes a Turn

In 2019, the work had become even more demanding and I was all consumed in my job. My average day started about 5:00 AM and continued well past 6:30 or 7:00 PM most evenings. I was also on call for any emergencies and there were unfortunately many of them. It was not unusual for me to be on calls through the nights and weekends. I felt like I was working non-stop. Our global CIO left the company early in 2019 and I was asked to stand in as the Global CIO while they filled the position permanently. I am not one who seeks the highest ranks so I was not really interested in holding the position permanently, but I agreed to cover while they found the right fit. It was a humbling experience and I embraced the role as best I knew how. Through relationships. The previous CIO had a challenging history with a lot of the other management team so I came in to build bridges. It's what I do and it's what I love. I met so many new people and learned so much about them, their dreams and goals and how they thought the company should move forward. But most of them were in Europe. I flew the equivalent of 4 times around the world that year!

The Career Takes a Turn

When you know the names of the flight attendants on the overseas trips to Europe, you are traveling too much!

Even though I had been in Senior Management for a long time, I had no idea what kind of pressure these senior executives are under. It was the most demanding role I have ever held and it opened my eyes to the real politics behind corporations. You don't want to be there if you want to keep your sanity and your soul. You find yourself doing things and saying things that may not really represent who you are inside. But you plow through as best you can. I had a friend and co-worker at the time that was on my previous team and she was the wind beneath my wings. As true friends always do, she stepped in and took control of my previous team, making sure that they had all they needed and were well cared for when I could not be there. She is the type of person that can take any task and run with it without need of direction. It was easier for her though, since everyone already had great respect for her. But the thing I remember most is that, not only did she look after my team, she also looked after me. Any time I needed someone to discuss ideas with, have a non-work-related conversation or just a shoulder to cry on, she was there for me 100%. Again, true friends can see you through the best of times and the worst of times.

If I thought I was working a lot of hours before the interim position, I was surprised to find that it didn't come close to my work schedule now. Distractions aside, it was the most demanding part of my career. The rewards were great in that I met so many new people and gained so much insight. And it was also the continued distraction from still trying to get over the passing of Willa and Maggie, which remained at the forefront of most of my days, albeit silently.

My company pays out the yearly bonus in April and when I got my bonus that year, I was finally able to pay off the second mortgage on the house. Like I said, I had a plan to get back to better than abundant and this was a big piece of the plan. And even though it was years after the divorce, it was one of the most satisfying events of that year. Paying off the second mortgage was the last piece of the debt reduction plan and with that, I was finally in a position to celebrate and start planning for the future, specifically what I would do about retirement. I had little to no savings at this point and was really starting to get concerned about my retirement plan and lack of any nest egg to start that planning. But like all of the other times, I began to save money and find an investment counselor to help me. If you are like me, it seems a little silly to find an investment counselor when you don't really have any money to invest! But it's planting the seeds to the growth and wealth that is meant to come. To shine the focus on saving and to begin to attract that into my life – abundance, it is a mindset, remember?

I still spent time with my best friend and enjoyed that immensely. We went to a wine tasting class one weekend afternoon and enjoyed discovering lots of delicious wine from Italy. As we sat and sipped, we started talking about how much fun it would be to go to Italy and really see the wineries and feel that magic. Neither of us were in a place financially where we should be talking about a trip to Italy, but we looked at options and I used my airline miles to cover the business class tickets to Rome. So off we went, for 10 glorious days in Italy. It was truly the trip of a lifetime. We toured most of Italy and were on the road quite a lot. We went with a tour group and the people we met were wonderful and fun.

FABULOUS

The most amazing part of the trip for me was the opportunity to visit Assisi. I have always greatly admired St. Francis for his love of nature and animals and for the wonderful "Simple Prayer" that he wrote. We had the opportunity to visit the huge Basilica of St. Francis and the Church of St. Mary of the Angels, noted for the place of St. Francis' death. It was a humbling and very emotional experience to see the beautiful frescos and feel the peace and love of that place. We were led downstairs to a small sanctuary where they had some prayer candles you could use and then keep for yourself. I picked one up and was immediately overwhelmed with thoughts and feelings of Willa and Maggie and how I could really feel their spirits there with me. I cried for a while and it was both a cry of sadness and a cry of cleansing. I still have that candle and I light it every year for the girls to remember and connect with them through St. Francis. If you have never read St. Francis' prayer, I recommend you do. It's something we can all remember in our daily lives. And if you have never had the ultimate joy of visiting Italy, go! It is truly one of the most beautiful places in the world.

The Career Takes a Turn

Love Begins

It's funny, a friend of mine told me that after a divorce, it would be about a year or two before being ready to date again and start new relationships. I guess the Aquarian in me thought that was too soon and so I didn't open my heart to any relationship for eight years. But I was sitting on the couch one evening watching some show when I got pinged by a guy that I had dated in high school. He had reached out in the eight years before, but I had always ignored his messages. This particular evening, he said I was a bitch for not responding! Well, knowing that is NOT who I am at all, I messaged back to protest. He laughed and said that at least he got me to respond. We ended up talking on the phone for hours and I began to feel something stirring in my gut. It was a little refreshing and a little flattering to be pursued, especially by someone I had a relationship with in the past, albeit a really long time ago. But it made me more comfortable to open up since I knew him and trusted him. We had dated before, so there was something that I liked about him back then and thought maybe this could be a good thing.

We decided to meet at a restaurant near his house for drinks and dinner. I was so nervous but also a little intrigued to see how it would go. When I arrived, he was already there. It was summer and he was sitting out on the patio watching the band. I walked up and we greeted each other, although he would barely look at me. I thought that was kind of odd, but then I was so nervous I was just trying to get through the next few minutes. How did I look, what would I say, what would happen next? We went to dinner and had a good time catching up after all the years and we became more comfortable with each other. Then he told me why he wasn't looking at me earlier. He said that he could not believe how many wrinkles I had in my face! I was devastated, although of course tried not to show it. He even said that there were some really good plastic surgeons in town and it would only be a nip and a tuck to get rid of those wrinkles. It's really amazing how a comment like that will stay with you for years. I became completely self-conscious about my face and found my self-esteem dwindle more and more every time I looked in a mirror. Regardless, we dated for over six months and had some real fun together. However, the longer we were together I began to notice something within me that was resistant to the relationship. For one thing, I didn't like his music selection. It wasn't bad music, just not my taste. I was still into the 80's rock bands and he said that he was over that era of music and liked something a little quieter. He also had a little dog. I love dogs of all kinds and think I connect with most dogs, but the more time I spent with them, the more I realized I didn't really connect with his dog either. Music and animals. Finally, he had been dating someone else for a while before we started dating and he was having a hard time letting that other relationship go. Since I was not really serious about him, at least not yet, I was OK with him working through the relationship with the other woman. But when I returned from Italy and saw him again, the first words out of his mouth were that he had been with his old girlfriend while I was away. He said he could not resist her since she was so beautiful, oh but I was pretty too. Really? It was clear to me then that the relationship should end. I now know that our energies were not compatible but at the time, I just thought about how my pride was hurt and how annoying he had become. In general, Aquarians cannot be owned or controlled by any man and I felt like he was trying to control me. So, the relationship started to fade, even though he would still call and want to get together. I ultimately stopped seeing him and made the excuse that I had met someone else and wanted to pursue a relationship with the new guy, even though that wasn't exactly the whole truth. More on that later.

The Twins

FABULOUS

For many years, I have had numerous deer visit my secluded back yard and back woods. The mamas have come and gone, most times without me knowing what happened to them when they no longer came around. Each year, when it's time for the cutest baby deer you will ever see come into our world, I am blessed to be able to watch them grow up in the first year of life. This particular year, mama was ready to have her baby and so she came to my back yard woods, where she felt safe and loved. I was sitting on the upper deck when I saw her arrive and as I always do, I took a minute to just stop and watch. To my amazement, she birthed her baby right in the back yard woods! It was amazing to watch her lay down and instinctively know exactly what to do while her new fawn was brought into the world. When the fawn was born, she cleaned it and made sure that it was safe and cared for. When I thought it was all over, mama stopped and laid down again. And to my surprise she birthed her second baby! How fabulous to see two new little souls born into the world in my back yard woods. And again, as with the first one, she cleaned the second twin and made sure it also felt her love and protection. By this time, I couldn't keep my eyes off of this truly amazing event. After a few minutes, mama was resting (and with good reason) while the twins became oriented. Within the next hour, the twins were up and walking on very unstable legs but always only a few steps away from mama.

Now for those of you who don't know how fawns grow up in their first year, I will try and explain. The mamas have a scent that can be smelled by predators, while the babies don't yet have that scent. So, to protect the babies, the mamas will find a good camouflage place to leave the babies for the day. In the dawn hours, the mama comes to the babies and lets them nurse. It was particularly funny to watch the twins push and fight for space to nurse. Their little legs are not quite stable yet, so they fall and sway and lean, sometimes on each other. After breakfast, mama finds a place that she thinks is safe and she tells the baby, in this case babies, to lay down, be quiet, don't move, sleep and wait. She will bump their head so that they know this is their spot for the day. The babies lay down and blend so well with the surroundings that it's hard to see them, even when you know where they are. For the twins, one had a spot between a tree and the fence, covered in a clump of grass and the other had a spot a few feet over in another clump of grass. Then mama leaves to go find food and drink and get some rest. The twins lay in their spot all day, regardless of weather, and sleep, look around, and occasionally get up to stretch their legs, then lay right back down again. Then at dusk, mama comes back and makes a noise to let the twins know that she is there. The twins jump up and make the cutest "baaahing" sound because they are hungry and very glad to see mama! Mama feeds them and then she lovingly licks them all over and makes sure they are healthy and clean. After a while, she bonks them on the head again and tells them to lay down for the night while she goes back to the woods.

After the first few weeks, the twins started to spend time getting their "legs under them". I don't know if twin deer have the same soul connection as twin people do, but it sure looked like it from my seat. They spent a lot of time exploring their new world together and seeing who could get to mama fastest when she arrived. I had to laugh when I saw mama, because by now she looked like she could use a vacation from the twins. The twins began to have a little more freedom to roam around during the day and mama would spend more time with them in the back yard woods. It always broke my heart though when mama would go over the fence and leave the twins. They would run and pace up and down the fence line with the most mournful "baaahing" to try and coax her back. Eventually I put a gate in and left it open so the twins could go back and forth with mama, even though it took them a while to figure out where the gate was. By this time the twins really had their legs and that's when the fun really started. They would be hanging out with mama and the other deer, and then all of the sudden they would jump up and start running as fast as they could around the yard. They didn't know where they were going but they would chase each other, run, jump, fall down and get right back up to do it all over again. To see these two little angels, with their little white fawn spots, play so hard was hilarious! At times I was crying from laughing so hard at them. When they got going, all of the rabbits, squirrels and other deer just got out of the way or else be trampled in the fun.

The Twins

As an animal totem, the deer symbolizes family protection, gentleness, intuitiveness and innocence. You can call on the deer spirit when you need some strength to get through a difficult time in your life. (*Animal Spirit Guides* by Steven D. Farmer, Ph.D.)

The Aging Parents

My parents were now in their nineties and amazing that they were still able to mostly live independently. With some help along the way, they continued to live in the home that I grew up in. I coordinated some in-home care several times for them and we had talked about them moving into a retirement community but the conversation usually stopped pretty quickly. I had looked at several places that I thought would be a fit for them. The goal was to remove the obligation of keeping up a house and yard, getting proper hot meals and having reliable transportation to the store and doctor visits so my mom would not have to drive. My dad had been losing his vision for years and he was almost legally blind by then, so it was also important to find a place that could help him compensate for his vision loss. Finally, it was important to me that they had new friends who they could spend time with and enjoy their later years. I was at their house one weekend when they said that they had been talking and thinking about moving into that retirement home and that they were ready to look at some places. I was amazed at their decision and told them that I would help them get through the selection process for a new location, guide them through the move itself and take care of selling their house. I know a lot of you have been through a similar experience and so you can relate to the work and planning it takes to embark on a move like this. We looked at numerous places before deciding on one near my home and we signed the papers for them to move into a villa on the retirement home property. This would give them a little more room and keep them from having to move into an apartment, which my mom was very much against. So, after months of planning and packing, we moved them to their new home in November. The move went smoothly and they tried to settle in to the new place. Meanwhile, we got the old home ready to be sold. Cleaning out a house that someone has lived in for 60 years is both daunting and humbling. But we got through the clean up and put the old house on the market. Meanwhile, I would visit mom and dad as much as possible to make sure they were settling in and getting what they needed. The retirement home provided three meals a day and that was one of the things I was so excited about, so that mom would not feel the need to cook any longer. But she had other plans. Each time I would ask about the meals, there was a reason why they chose not to take advantage of them. One of those reasons was that the dining room was in the main building and they were in the villa, so they would have to walk or drive to the dining room. And that seemed to be an overwhelming task. So, I worked with them to have the meals delivered to the villa instead. That wasn't much better. Either the timing was off, the food was cold or they didn't want what was on the menu. It broke my heart more and more each time I went to see them because they were both becoming stressed and unhappy with the set up. But we tried to make it work as best we could. Then, about a month after they moved in, I was over there to help with groceries and cleaning and my dad asked if we could go for a walk. I said of course! It was a beautiful sunny day even for late November and I always love to be outdoors. We loaded him into his electric wheelchair and we took the dog out for a walk. About half-way through the walk, my dad confessed that he was unhappy but that mom was devastated about moving. The stress on her had become very obvious and you could see it in her face, hear it in her voice and feel it in her mood. He said that he was so concerned that if they did not move back home, this place would kill her. And that he felt so guilty even saying this after everything we had done to make this happen. I guess he was really surprised when I told him that this was not a punishment and that if they wanted to move back to the house then it was absolutely OK and I would make all of the arrangements. The great thing about my relationship with my parents at this point was that we could talk about tough subjects and speak the truth about what we thought. When we returned to the villa, I told mom what dad and I talked about and asked her if she was OK with moving back to their old home. She was overjoyed, yet also carried that same guilt that dad talked about. I was not able to relieve their guilt, because in truth, you cannot relieve anyone else's guilt or sorrow or pain, but I was able to get them moved back into their home a month after they had moved out. We didn't even have to tell the movers where the furniture needed to go since they had just been there a month before! They settled back in quickly and their mood changed dramatically. It was the right thing to do.

The Following Year

The following year continued much like the one before. At work, the new CIO was put in place and I was able to go back to my "old" job with less stress even though the hours of work didn't really change. I worked from home mostly at this point and began to like not having to commute to work each day, but I missed the face to face with my folks and did my best to keep up with everyone through virtual meetings. I also continued riding with my friends and we had some great fun on the bikes. I was beginning to feel more and more that I might like to be able to ride on my own instead of always depending on my friends for a ride. Then my friend said he had an acquaintance who wanted to sell his motorcycle, and I was all in! Gorgeous bike that just needed a little love – black and chrome shiny! I thought that this would be the perfect smaller bike to learn to ride. As I always do, I dove into training, learning about how to handle a bike, online classes and reading books. I took the drivers written test and passed with flying colors and even got a temporary motorcycle endorsement on my driver's license! I was finally ready to go to the road school. I enrolled in a riding academy near my house and could not wait for the class to come. It was a weekend class that started on Friday evening. There were only 6 of us in the class so it was small and friendly and everyone was so excited about riding. I was the only female though, surprise, surprise. I went to the class on Friday evening and it was mostly about what would happen in the next two days and basic riding skills – a lot of what we had learned online before this class so I was feeling really good about my level of knowledge. Saturday morning came and we all showed up in full gear and ready to go. It was summertime and really hot once the sun came up but we were so excited, we didn't mind the heat. The riding academy supplies their own motorcycles for the class, so the instructor got everyone their bike and helped us walk them out to the training course. Wow were these things big and heavy!!!! As I took over walking the bike the rest of the way, I hit my shin bones about 100 times and was starting to heat up in the sun. But I couldn't wait to get going. We started in formation and just walked the bikes around for a bit, practiced starting them up and using the clutch and brakes. It was so much fun! Then we were ready to start to actually ride. We were just supposed to go across the short part of the training area and stop. And we were supposed to start lifting our feet off the ground and on to the bike. Hmmmmm. Seems I had a little problem with balance. Every time I tried to lift my feet, my bike would lean to one side or the other and I would have to put my feet down again. The other guys were getting it really fast, which didn't help with my self-esteem that was now beginning to fade rapidly. But I kept a smile as much as possible and wiped the sweat away as I tried again. At break time, the instructor sent the guys back in for a cool drink and asked if I wanted some one-on-one training time – which I graciously accepted even though inside I was now mortified that I couldn't do this. We worked for another 20 minutes but I don't think it actually really helped. He let me go in for a drink and as soon as I sat down to rest for a minute, it was time to go back out since the other guys had already been on break the entire time I was getting my private lesson. We all went back out and lined up to start again, this time we were all in a circle. The training exercise now was learning to turn. We would ride for a few feet until the next turn in the circle, always controlled and slow. As I rolled up to the first leg of the course, I tried picking my feet up and lost control of the bike. I dropped the bike to the ground, but wasn't hurt, at least not physically. Mentally I was so embarrassed I could hardly look at the instructor. He was so kind though and he came over to assist me in getting the bike back up and me back on the bike. We talked a bit about what happened and why I dropped the bike but at this point I don't think I heard a word he said. When it was my time to go again, I had even forgotten how to start the bike. Fear breeds more fear and I was gaining fear leaps and bounds. He walked back over to talk me through the startup sequence again and help calm me down. I am 100% sure he saw that fear in my eyes. As I started around the track again, this time I was on the section next to the woods. I took a deep breath and started forward and like each time before, when I picked up my feet, the bike leaned over. I was exhausted from handling this beast of a bike and I was so hot I could hardly breathe, so naturally when the bike tipped, it went over again, this time heading straight for the woods! Oh boy, did I ever feel mortified! I laid there on the ground with the bike until the instructor came over and helped me get up. He asked me what went wrong and of course I had no idea and was now barely able to even speak without bursting into tears. But he was very kind. As he helped me back on the bike, he looked me straight in the eyes and said "Are you sure you really want to do this"? *Wow*. The decision moment came and I thought about it for a couple of seconds before I said, "No, I'm not sure I want to do this". He told me I could start practicing on a smaller bike with other people who rode and then I could come back to the class when I felt I was ready. I agreed and slowly turned around, walked back to the office, gathered my things and drove home. I was so disappointed. When I got home, I changed clothes and went outside to sit on the patio and lick my wounds. And then I cried for hours. Something that was so very important to me and new in my life and I was a complete failure. I had also made a fool of myself in the class (at least that's what my ego was telling me). No one from the class really thought poorly of me but remember that lens I talked about earlier – well my lens was pointed directly at me and what an absolute failure I was. I have a really hard time with being laughed at or put down or embarrassed and it is still one of the things I am working on to understand it, forgive and love myself and let it go. So, I moped around the rest of the day, had to tell my friends that I "flunked" the class and then figure out what was next. By Sunday, I had come to the realization that being a passenger isn't such a bad thing after all. I would always have someone to ride with, I could enjoy the scenery and the beauty of the open road and I could do some filming! Yes, maybe that is a massive rationalization but it worked for me at the time. I still own that sportster and I still ride as a passenger and I still love it that way. But I leave open the possibility that I may one day want to learn to ride on my own and when that day comes, it will be a completely different experience, guaranteed.

We continued to ride that year and had lots of fun trips to the mountains and the beach. I grew to love it even more, especially when you get to ride curves like the Dragon's Tail in the North Carolina mountains. That is a thrill that stays with you always!

The Following Year

In December, my best friend and I were trying to decide what we would do for Christmas. I had abandoned Christmas with the family and my friend was single and wanted to get away as well. We decided that we would spend Christmas in Savannah. I think we all have an affinity for certain places. They seem to have a vibe that

61

resonates deep within us and makes us feel wonderful. For me, that city is Savannah, Georgia. I visited Savannah many, many years before and really fell in love with the place. I had not been back to Savannah since, so we decided that would be a great place to spend Christmas. We rented a quaint house near the river and we had a great time. When you can spend hours and hours with someone just talking about anything and everything, you know that you are truly compatible. And we spent a lot of time just hanging out and talking. It was fabulous. True friends are such a special gift. The house had a wonderful enclosed courtyard as a lot of Savannah homes do, and even in the chill, I would sit outside and just take in the beauty and peace of this lovely courtyard. I was inspired by the gorgeous Spanish moss swaying in the wind, the beautiful brick courtyard and the offset fence. It was covered in ivy and had special little trinkets that the home owner had placed around the garden. Clearly those trinkets meant something to them. It was so special how they were woven throughout the ivy all around the garden. What a magical place!

The Savannah Garden

When we returned home, I wanted to have that special feeling at my own house so I could go back to that peaceful place in my heart. There was a section of my yard that was getting worse by the year with erosion and I was desperate to find an answer to this eye sore. As I mused over the numerous options of what to do with this small part of my yard, my intuition led me back to the pictures I had taken of the courtyard in Savannah. That's what I wanted! So, I planned out the whole thing on paper, got the fence guys to come and put in a beautiful privacy fence, hired a brick mason to lay the patio with red brick that looked weathered but loved and of course, I had to have the Bird Girl statue that used to stand in Bonaventure Cemetery in Savannah. I bought a replica of the statue and had the brick mason permanently seat it in the middle of the new garden. There was an area for planting on both sides of the brick patio and I launched into the garden plan for what to include. The first "must haves" were saga palms, the beautiful, luxurious palms that lined the streets of Savannah. I added some azaleas and beautiful flowers and took advantage of the ivy that was already in the garden area to wrap the fence in a fabulous green blanket.

The Savannah Garden

Finally, I added a St. Francis statue and some little garden animal statues around the base to signify the love of peace and animals.

For the final touch, I ordered some Spanish moss and hung it from the trees in the garden. The Savannah Garden was glorious and I spent many long hours in the garden just being still and remembering great friends and great times. As the seasons change, tending to the Savannah Garden is my labor of love. I spend time pruning and weeding and sweeping and planting, many times forgetting everything else and losing myself there in pure bliss for hours and hours. I play the soundtrack from "Midnight in The Garden of Good and Evil" and enjoy the songs from Johnny Mercer, a native of Savannah. "Midnight in The Garden of Good and Evil" is a book and movie about Savannah and it is one of my all-time favorites. The Savannah Garden remains one of my sanctuaries and favorite places to be. Since deer won't jump a privacy fence, because they can't see the other side, I am able to plant anything I want, which is usually something the deer want as well, without the threat of it being eaten by the next day. Having a place of sanctuary is so important to living your best life and finding your center. For me, that's the Savannah Garden. For you, it could be anywhere. Even your favorite chair in the corner of a room. The point really is that you find the place that makes you so happy and content that you never want to leave. Use that place to just be still and listen. Meditate. Use it to find your inner peace. Use it to connect to your higher self that is within you and connect to the higher power of The Universe. Use it as your place to rest, rejuvenate, rejoice and relax. We all need that in our lives and The Universe wants you to find that part of yourself. So, build *your* Savannah Garden, use it to be happy and you will spread that happiness to others just by lighting up your own soul.

Yoga

As I was beginning to contemplate my upcoming retirement, I knew I would need activities that would not only occupy my time but also keep me physically active. With such expanding options through technology, I scrolled through some exercise shows on my smart TV and came across an introduction class to Yoga. I thought that would be a great thing to cover the time and physical intentions I had set out to address. But can I just say, WOW! What a fabulous way to blend the physical strengthening and stretching with the mind-body connection. Yoga is really about connecting to Universal Consciousness and achieving harmony within yourself. I started the 30-day introduction class and have never looked back. It is part of my daily routine now with meditation and visualization and it truly brings to life the spiritual practices that it supports. Yoga is also all about "active" stretching so you are engaging your muscles and nervous system constantly as you work through the various poses. It is about breath work and flow. I can say that my body is stronger and more flexible because of it. And that flexibility helps to prevent physical injuries as well. Yoga also taught me patience. Each day you take the poses a little further, without judgment, and you notice how your body feels in the flow from one pose to the other. It also teaches you balance so that you can be more stable in your physical body. It shows you how to be still in your body, mind and heart and increases the heart / brain connection which opens up the energy paths in your body to promote healing. And when you end your yoga practice with Anjali Mudra (bringing your palms together at your heart), you are expressing honor for yourself, your teacher, and The Universe as well as love and gratitude. And of course, you must have heard "namaste", which means honoring the divine light in each other, honoring the love, peace and truth in each other and knowing that we are one.

So, if you look at yoga as a metaphor for life, you can see that in life, we look for balance, strength, gratitude and love. We live without judgement of ourselves or others. We notice how our bodies feel, not good or bad, just have awareness. And find the time to be still and quiet and honor the light in others as they honor the light in you.

Meditation

I think meditation goes hand-in-hand with yoga. I have always believed that meditation was a great practice for anyone to do and I tried to start a practice of meditation many years ago. I read lots of books on how to do it and learned many different methods. The problem back then was that I didn't know why I was meditating. And when there is no reason, your mind starts to run in a thousand directions while you are trying to be still. I could never really make it work for me, so I stopped a short time after. Yes, that Aquarian thing kicked in again.

Today, meditation is an important part of my life and daily routine. And now I have a purpose. If you are starting meditation for the first time, be warned – there are thousands of books, websites and audios about how to meditate. Believe me I know! I was overwhelmed with all of this information when I started meditating again. Practically, what I have found over the past months is that all of the different approaches are great and you just need to find the one(s) that work for you. Some people are visual, some auditory and some sensory or feeling. I think that depending on what your strongest intuitive sense is, there are meditation practices that work better for each type of person. I have less success with "seeing" or visualizing when I meditate and most of the meditation work I have come across so far uses your ability to "see" in your mind's eye. So, when I use this type of meditation, I can get frustrated because I don't "see" what they are describing. I have found what works better for me is just background music and sounds or guided meditations that incorporate sound and emotion. Look around and explore what is available with your lens on and you can narrow down your preferences pretty quickly.

I also tend to do various types of meditations depending on how I feel that day and my energy level when I get up. Most people agree that morning meditation is great because your mind is only half-awake and you haven't started the barrage of ideas and to-do lists that your conscious mind is waiting to jump on. It's also agreed that evening meditation is great for setting the right mindset for a deep and peaceful sleep. And some people (me being one of them) use sleep meditations as well. But again, it's what works for you and only you.

For me, meditation is my best way to connect internally to my sub-conscious and outwardly to the quantum field or Universal Intelligence. Some days it's so easy to slip into the "zone" and feel so peaceful and disconnected from the world. Other days, it's almost impossible to turn off my conscious mind. On those days, I just put on my headphones and listen to some calming meditation sounds. But whatever that day of meditation brings, I always include time to just be grateful. Grateful for everything I have, grateful for all of the people who love me and for the people who don't. Grateful for what I can see that I already have in my mind, even if it is not yet manifested physically into my reality. Grateful for such a beautiful place to live, grateful for the unconditional love, grateful for infinite abundance and infinite health. And if I get additional messages or feelings during the session, then that's a bonus!

Of course, there are people who are extremely good at meditation and have been practicing it for decades. But even they have different practices and different results. And it's all grand. We learn so much from others if you take the time to ask, read about their work and listen to them speak. But the great thing I have found about meditation is that you don't have to be a guru to get great benefits from just being still for a few minutes and listening to your higher self. And the more you do it, the easier it gets. Your conscious mind will let go and allow you some time to be still, be creative, and turn down the stress in your life.

My hope is that you can set aside just a few minutes each morning or each evening, or both, and start practicing meditation. Find some guided meditations that resonate with you and use them as an example for how to do it on your own or just continue to use guided meditations. The important thing is that you are practicing how to use your breath and how to turn down your conscious mind.

Then, if you get stressed out during the day, you come back to that and just take a minute to do some dedicated breathing like you were doing during meditation. It will help you relax, think more clearly and reduce the impact of stress on your body. And who wouldn't want that!

Squirrels are So Funny!

I spend a lot of time outside on my patio just watching nature and I am always amazed by the squirrels. Most people I guess see them as little rodents and might consider them to be a nuisance because they eat all the birdseed and dig holes in all of our yards and flower beds. And in fact, I had to have my house "squirrel-proofed" because they kept chewing holes in my roof line to get into the attic! But if you spend time really watching them, you'll be amazed and amused at what you really see. Squirrels are the most playful creatures and they so love playing chase through the yard with each other, up the trees, jumping from branch to branch as if the leader is forging the obstacle course and all of the others have to follow. But even when they are alone, they rejoice in stopping for a few minutes from gathering dinner or building a new nest and just enjoy their life. I had an old dog toy, a little stuffed ball, in the back yard woods that I couldn't bear to throw away, so it stayed there through the years to remind me of my Berners. A little squirrel found it one day and decided to play ball with himself. He crept up on the stuffed toy and then pounced with all fours on top of the ball and rolled around in the leaves while he grasped that ball with all his might. He would roll around for a while, then drop the ball and run off, only to come back with even more spunk and pounce on the ball again and roll around on the ground. He was having the most fabulous time and you could literally feel the fun and excitement he had rolling, dropping, running and coming back for more. I literally laughed out loud as I watched him play and play and keep coming back for more. It really makes your heart sing when you are part of a universe where the animals haven't forgotten that we were meant to play and have fun and rejoice in the small joys that we have every day. It doesn't take a lot of time, but the way it makes you feel is indescribable. And it doesn't take a lot. My little squirrel only had an old dog toy. I've also seen them do that with pine cones or sticks. When you have pure joy in your heart, as that little squirrel did, anything can make you happy. If you give yourself permission to laugh and play and be creative and have fun, even if only for 20 minutes, your entire perspective changes for the rest of the day. As an animal totem, the squirrel represents preparedness, strategic thinking, speed, abundance and is upbeat, playful and joyous. Call on the squirrel spirit when "you want to focus your energies so that you're more purposeful and directed". (*Animal Spirit Guides* by Steven D. Farmer. Ph.D.)

My Soulmate (?)

In February of the following year, I was "re-connected" with an old friend of the male persuasion. Remember when I said that when I was trying to let go of the other guy, I told him I had started dating someone else? Well, in my mind, that person was this friend. I had known him for a few years and was always very attracted to him and loved to spend time with him. We could talk for hours and there was a kindred-soul feeling I think for both of us. I would see him occasionally through the years and was always so excited when the opportunity came along. We would always greet each other in a big warm hug that you could feel down to your toes. So, around this time, I saw him and made the bold move to ask him to come over sometime. Much to my great surprise, he texted me a few weeks later and said he had the day off and asked if I was around. My response: Of course!!!!! As circumstances would have it, I was actually off from work that day and told him I would love to see him. So, he came over. We spent the entire morning and most of the afternoon just talking – about anything and everything. I found we had a tremendous number of things in common and it was just so easy to be around him. The afternoon flew by as we talked and laughed and got to know each other. When he left, we made plans for him to come back a couple of days later. I was really on top of the world! To finally have had the kind of quality time we had together and find that indeed there was something between us solidified what I had "known" for the past few years. We were very compatible and so comfortable with each other. It really felt like we were soulmates. I floated through the next few days on the greatest high until he came back. When he came over, the hug was even better and the conversation was more engaging. And as the afternoon went on, we became romantic. And when I thought my excitement could not be any higher, the connection we forged was beyond anything I could have imagined. This was the kind of connection where your skin tingles, your heart races and your spirit soars. I had never had this type of connection with anyone in my life. I could not stop thinking about him nor could I remove the smile from my face. It was pure magic.

And then it wasn't. He went radio silence.

Of course, like most people would do I guess, I assumed it was me and something I did or didn't say, or something I did or didn't do. I reached out a few times but he would not respond. And as each day passed, the self-doubt grew to proportions that I had never known in my life. I was completely devastated. The tears I cried for my dogs became tears I cried for this failed relationship. And boy did I cry. I cried myself to sleep almost every night and it just grew more and more painful. I could compartmentalize it during the day because my work was still so demanding but each night, the pain and loneliness and self-doubt would return for another punch in the gut.

And the music supported my mood. It was so sad and depressing, full of songs about lost love, aloneness and yes, even suicide. I would sit outside each evening and wallow in the sad music.

But the deer still came every day and they gave me hope and even made me smile every now and then. And the birds still sang and the squirrels still played.

This went on for six months. I was a complete mess of a human being. But life drives you forward and so it did for me as well. Work was becoming extremely demanding with organizational reorgs, impossible projects and long, long days. I had times during some of the video conference calls where I just broke down into tears and had to hang up. The stress levels were off the charts and there was no end in sight of that changing. I spent a lot of time in the Savannah Garden and it was a great relief to forget about everything except Mother Earth. I planted, tilled the soil, cleaned up the pine cones and then just sat and enjoyed the tranquility. By July, I was convinced that I would never see him again and forced myself to take baby steps to move forward. So, I joined a dating site for bikers. I figured that I might as well find a new love and one that shared my love of motorcycle-riding. I had not been on a dating site since before I was married and wow had things changed! For me, it was a super boost to the ego for the first few weeks. I would log in about once a day and have lots of pings and likes and requests. I thought perhaps I could make it through the depression with that kind of attention. It was actually really fun! I was having trouble committing to actually meeting anyone however and so I didn't push it too hard. Then I connected with a super nice guy who seemed genuine and so we set up a phone call. We talked for a long time and it was really nice. The next morning, he texted me with a very sweet hello and I was feeling like maybe I could be happy again and make something new work. And then he texted me again, and again, and again over the next few days. It went from sweet to smothering. I stopped responding all together even though we had planned to meet for a ride. I felt awful for doing that but I literally had a physical adverse reaction to the constant flow of communication. A couple of days went by and he texted that he didn't understand where I had gone and why I went radio silent. BOING! I was doing to him what my "soulmate" had done to me and so I knew how that must feel. *Horrible!* I dug deep down inside and gathered the courage to call him and explain what I was feeling and that it seemed that maybe I was not really ready to date after all. He was so kind and understanding and was also so grateful that I had called to explain instead of leaving him wondering. A good lesson for all of us – most people need closure and, in most cases, would prefer to hear the hard truth than not hear anything at all (even if it's not what they want to hear). This is a life lesson that I continue to learn even to this day.

At this point, I decided that a biker dating site probably wasn't the right path for me and I removed myself from the site. It was the right decision at the time, but it reignited that old, seeping wound and the pain and loneliness were magnified once more. I would fantasize about what I would do or say if I ever saw my soulmate again. Some days those fantasies were ugly and hateful and I could envision myself slapping him and slamming the door in his face. Other days those fantasies were complete forgiveness and there was left only love. But in reality, I couldn't know what I would do in that moment, or if that moment would ever present itself anyway. I was so depressed one evening that the emotions almost took me over. The anguish I felt was so real that I could not stop the open sobbing and I screamed out to the world – "what did I do wrong and why did you leave without a trace"!!!! Fists pumping, tears streaming, almost hyperventilating, I finally fell into a fitful sleep.

Little did I realize at the time that the emotional state I was in was so strong that I was manifesting him back into my life.

The next morning, I was on a conference call for work and he texted me. I almost fell out of my chair! And the message was not about the things that I did wrong or what was wrong with me, but about his emotional struggle with himself, where he was personally and our relationship. It was quite a long text and it was very sincere. He apologized several times for ghosting me and asked if there was anything he could do to make the situation better. So here I am on a conference call that I need to be paying attention to and trying to read this text at the same time. I had to read it in spurts because of the call so it was hard to piece it all together. After my call ended, I must have read it 50 times before I responded. But it was clear from the second read that my response would be the one of complete forgiveness. I weighed the options and came to the conclusion that clearly what I wanted was him, so why would I even for a minute consider any vengeful or hateful response and then jeopardize the ONE thing I had wanted for the past six months – to see him again. And in that instant moment of decision, the happiness that flowed over me replaced all of the hate, self-doubt and misery I had been living with for half a year. I responded with a message of complete forgiveness and told him my door was always open. We made plans to see each other that weekend. When he came over, we talked about what happened and where he was emotionally. And as it normally went with us, we mostly laughed about the whole thing. However, I did not share the deep anguish I had been going through for the past six months. For what reason, I don't know. But I did make a firm demand – no matter what happens going forward, he had to tell me when his feelings changed and whatever he did, he could not ghost me again like that. He agreed.

FABULOUS

Little did I know that this would be the start of the final phase of my awakening.

More to come.

COVID

Since this was all happening in 2020 and 2021, you know the biggest thing on everyone's mind was COVID. UGH. Well, for me, COVID is just another virus. You may have noticed that nowhere in this dialogue have I mentioned me being sick. That's because I haven't been sick in over a decade. In fact, I haven't even been to a doctor. You have no idea how really powerful your thoughts are and I did not do this manifestation purposefully, but more out of need. As you know, I am extremely independent. When I became single again, I told myself over and over that I could no longer get sick from ANYTHING because I didn't have anyone to take care of me. Even though that was a powerful manifestation, perhaps it was done for the wrong reasons.

Be that as it may, I really am never sick nor do I believe that being exposed to a virus automatically means you will contract it. But if you live in fear of getting sick, and you listen to the pharms and the doctors and the news tell you that you will be sick with something: COVID, cancer, diabetes, heart disease, allergies, and sadly the list goes on and on, then surely you will manifest any number of illnesses to meet your individual stresses and fears. Now, I know that may sound harsh to some people, but if you understand that your thoughts and actions drive everything that happens in your human life here on this planet, then you can also understand that you have THE ABILITY to change any of it. 100%. I believe that you can cure your body of any of these dis-eases and that has been proven over and over again from ancient wisdoms and civilizations to modern teachings. If you are suffering from any dis-ease, please seek out help other than your Western-trained doctor. I believe the combination of Western medicine and Eastern medicine is the best balance of both and it only takes you reaching inside yourself to find the cure and be whole again. Universal Consciousness wants you to be healthy and to live in love. But it's hard to be happy when you are sick with dis-ease. PLEASE do not underestimate the power of your body to heal itself and please seek out ways to do that. It could mean your life after all. And I am not saying this from a "flaky" Aquarian perspective where I believe in everything. There is scientific evidence of this now as well as real people curing themselves every day. And it all starts with your consciousness and energy.

I did get the COVID vaccine because I was still traveling for work and I felt I had to do that in order to meet the needs and requirements of my company. But if I knew then what I know now, that choice probably would have been different. However, there are no regrets and everything you do is part of your journey. You can be safe in the knowledge that where you are right now and what you are doing is perfect for the present moment. You are divine and therefore what you do is also of the divine.

The Story Continues

At this point, 2021 looked like it would be a great year. Things were really good. My "soulmate" and I were spending time together and it was a very happy part of my life. Work was busy and I was now thinking about when I would retire. I continued to ride motorcycles as often as I could and enjoy time with my family and friends. I enjoyed spending time in the Savannah Garden and always found peace there. The deer came on a daily basis and continued to bring new little ones into the world. What a joy to see all of the animals thriving. It seemed that things couldn't get much better.

By this time the music had turned 180 degrees again. Instead of the sad, soulful songs, it was now fun, sexy rock and roll with Aerosmith, Def Leppard, Lynyrd Skynyrd and some Meatloaf thrown in for good measure. Life was rockin'!

My "soulmate" would occasionally need financial support, so I was happy to help with that and gave him funds through the months when he needed it. It always made me feel good to be able to help him even though

I think it made him feel badly at times. But one of the Aquarian traits is that we can't say no to someone in need. It's like a compulsion. Even when I thought it could be on the verge of excessive, I was literally unable to say no anytime he had a need. I was eager to make this relationship all it could be and I started researching astrology to guide me. I discovered a site that did compatibility readings based on birthdate and time and I ordered one for us. (www.compatible-astrology.com). It was really amazing. The reading came in three parts: One about the relationship and how we interact together and then one for each of us individually. Wow! Was it ever accurate. I learned a lot and it reminded me of things I had forgotten about myself that I had known in the past. It also talked about the extremely strong attraction that we had for each other but also pointed out the things that may not work between us. Overall, it was very encouraging though and I tried to use the information to help us be better together. I did not tell him that I had ordered this though. I was embarrassed I guess to admit to believing in something like that and I didn't want to jeopardize anything between us.

At this point in my career, I was sure I needed to move on and get out of the corporate rat race. The pressure was becoming too much and the hours were too long. I discussed my situation with my boss and we mutually decided that I would retire in April. It was a year earlier than I had planned, but after reviewing where I was mentally, it was the right decision for sure. As we talked through all of this, he introduced me to something called "Notes from the Universe" by Mike Dooley (www.tut.com). I signed up to receive email notes from The Universe each weekday and it literally changed my life forever. They are the most uplifting messages and I found myself looking for this email every morning first thing before work. It is still one of my great joys each day. If you would like to be inspired and feel Universal love, go to www.TUT.com and sign up. Maybe it will change your life too.

The Beginning of the Beginning

One afternoon in February, my "soulmate" texted me to see if I was home. I had not seen him in some time due to his travel and the holiday schedules we both had. At this point, my work days were getting easier and easier with the upcoming retirement so I had time to spend with him. When he came over, he told me he was moving out of state. I was so shocked that I didn't know how to respond. Inside I was crushed to the core, but outwardly to him I was happy he had a great new opportunity. And in fact, I guess I actually felt both of those things. I never really envisioned a long-term thing with him because we were so different with where we were in our lives, but I didn't want to hear that it would be over so soon. We spent one last afternoon together and when he left, I was numb. I had finally found someone that made me so happy and now that was over. We had talked about staying in touch, but I knew that was just talk to ease the separation. The split was easier to deal with this time however, because it was something that was good for him and he was open and honest. And it wasn't him making a deliberate decision to not see me anymore. I found some solace in that.

I stayed busy with weekend bike rides and various bike week trips with my friends. I was also doing a final tour of my work locations to say my good-byes to everyone before I retired. It was very gratifying to see the love and thanks from everyone. Though I was so happy to be starting a new phase of my life, it was difficult to say good-bye to such fabulous people, some I had known for more than a decade. As retirements go, this was a blueprint for how to do it right. I left with such joy and love in my heart from the outpouring of my friends and co-workers.

My college girlfriends and I had planned a trip to the mountains for a long weekend right after my last day. It was such a great trip! It warms my heart to be with these wonderful women and to see their accomplishments and feel a sense of wholeness that is hard to come by except for friends that you have known for almost 40 years. Can you imagine! I think we all must have decided to take this life adventure together before we came to Earth because it feels like old souls who just love to play together.

While I was there, my "soulmate" texted to tell me that his move had been delayed and he could use some funds to help with the situation. We planned to see each other when I got back home. I was overjoyed to be able to see him again, even knowing that it was probably the last time I would have that chance. I will freely admit though that at this point, I was feeling less happy about the money. My ego was moving into overdrive and I started feeling that perhaps that was one of the main reasons he was seeing me. Of course, we all have egos that make up stories when we listen to it too much. But again, I was incapable of saying no.

A bike rally drew me away for a week but we had a fabulous time! I always so love to go to the bike rallies. There is no other kind of people watching like people at a bike rally, hahaha. You can sit for hours and just be amazed at what you see. There is very little left to the imagination and sometimes that's not a good thing. But it is the best feeling to just ride for hours and have the opportunity to be one with nature and your thoughts. And I sure was spending a lot of time thinking about my "soulmate".

The next bike trip was to the beach. It is a gorgeous place with lots of history and great places to ride. My friends and I left early in the afternoon for our 6-hour ride, me still a passenger. Weather was good and we were enjoying the sights along the way. As we were heading down the highway, my friend pulled up beside us on her bike and said that she thought something might be wrong. We looked over to see that her front tire was almost completely flat! She could not see it herself of course but she could certainly feel it in the way the bike handled. We immediately pulled off the next exit in a little small town in the middle of nowhere. We saw a small convenience store and pulled into the parking lot. As we examined her bike, for sure the tire was totally flat. We tried using some tire goo to inflate it, but when she got back on the bike to test it, the tire goo was oozing out of the rim all over the tire! It was a goner. Of course, you can't carry spare tires on a bike, so we were stuck. It was Memorial Day weekend and getting dark at this point. Nothing was open nearby to help with getting a new tire, so we called for a tow. That was a complete disaster. The tow company promised that someone would come in a few hours (that would put us at midnight) and it was about 9:00 PM now. We called the local police department to inform them that we were camped out at the convenience store in case something happened. The police were very kind and stopped by to check on us a couple of times. They even brought us some bottled water! So, without being able to do anything else, we pulled out the tablet and watched a movie! Make lemonade, as they say! At midnight, there was still no tow, so we called back to find that they had cancelled the request because they could not find anyone to come out on Memorial Day weekend at midnight! Oh my! Would we be stuck sleeping in the parking lot all night? We called the police back and they came over to help. We had tried calling all of the local tow companies we could find in the area but no one would answer the phone call. So, the police officer said he could reach out to their emergency tow company and see if they would come. At this point, all we wanted was to get to a hotel to spend the rest of the night and regroup in the morning. When the police called, the tow company answered and agreed to come get us and take us to the next town. Whew! We checked in to the hotel at 2:30 AM, so grateful that we had a place to sleep and shower. The next morning, we called the tow company that had cancelled the call from the night before and they were there within the hour. Hmmmm. But we were finally on our way to the beach! And we had a ball the rest of the time we were there. I texted my "soulmate" during the week but the response was very short. I wasn't feeling the soul love.

When we got back from the trip, I had a one-week consulting opportunity so I was gone again. Even being retired, my friends knew that I would always help them when they needed me and this was a pretty nice gig in a really nice place! On the trip I was privileged to have a young female travel partner who went with me to learn and assist. We hit it off instantly and had a fabulous time working together as well as taking some leisure time. What a gorgeous place! We talked, laughed and ate and drank our way through a wonderful sight-seeing adventure and became fast friends. One of my joys in my life is mentoring others and she soaked it all up like a sponge. It was a glorious week! The day before we were set to come home, my "soulmate" texted me that he had additional problems financially and needed some additional money. And of course, I told him I would help him when I returned home. He came over the next day to get a check and it was a strange time. Before he left, we hugged, as we always did, but this time it was such a deeper hug and we held each other so long and so tight and I could feel that the end was here. It is one of my fondest memories of him and when you talk about emotion, that was an emotion I will likely never forget. We texted some back and forth after that but I could feel him pulling away more and more. He began to miss dates where we said we would meet with some excuse or another and I knew it was all finally coming to a close.

One afternoon in the following weeks, he texted me again with a heartfelt, long text asking for a loan. And it was not an insignificant amount of money. And even though I had promised myself that I would not support him any longer financially, I, of course, was incapable of saying no, *again*. So, he came over to get the funds and it was the most distant we had ever been with each other. He did set up a payment plan to pay me back and since I trusted him implicitly, I did not insist on any paperwork to detail the loan or the pay back. He said he would come back at the end of the week when he had more time to spend with me. He didn't show. And he didn't text to say he wasn't coming.

Can you say, BIG RED FLAG!

Coffee with Mr. Turtle

One of the best mornings I had since I retired was with Mr. Turtle. I was sitting at the kitchen table having my first cup of coffee and I looked out of the large picture window in my kitchen and saw a little box turtle in the yard heading over to the Savannah Garden. I was so happy to see him because I hadn't seen a turtle in a long time and I love them.

I watched the little guy slowly make his way across the grass, taking stops along the way to feel and smell and see what was in his path. I'm not sure what his destination was as he seemed to wander a bit but whether on purpose or not, he was making his way to the gate of the Savannah Garden. By the time he had made it across the yard, I was on my second cup of coffee. Turtles don't move very quickly, hahaha. There is a small step up to enter the garden and as he approached the step, he stopped and assessed what he would do. To my surprise, he headed straight for the step and moved forward to step up. I smiled at Mr. Turtle, admiring his bravery to move forward to what must have looked like a mountain in front of him. But he forged ahead and started to climb the step. He made it about half way before he lost his balance and fell from the step to the ground below and tipped over. I held my breath because I was so engrossed in watching this little guy forge ahead to make his way to where ever he thought he should be. But as all turtles do, he adjusted, regrouped, righted himself and then moved on as if nothing had happened. But he took a different path to the woods from there so he wouldn't have to climb the mountain again. I smiled and laughed at my little friend the turtle.

So, what's the point of this silly little morning coffee story? The turtle didn't see that falling off the step was a mistake, a problem or something to rock his world, but merely a bump in his road that was easily overcome. He simply picked himself up and moved on. Animals have an amazing ability to not let ego or pride or disappointment put up walls to what and where they want to go. They are so tuned in and filled with the universal spirit that obstacles are not deterrents. It made me think about how I would have reacted had something like that happened to me first thing in the morning on the way to work or starting my day and like a lot of people, I could let it literally ruin my whole day. I'd be grumpy and mad and I would be sending that vibration out into the world everywhere I went. So, if you think about it, if a turtle can be brave enough to move forward after running into and falling off a mountain, how bad can it be to have a little bump in the road sometime in the day and not think about that little turtle and just laugh. Because in the end, you probably didn't fall off a mountain.

As an animal totem, the turtle represents determination, staying grounded and being persistent. I think we can all appreciate those characteristics as we forge ahead with our lives. Call on the turtle spirit if you need some help with staying the course and slowing your hectic life down. (*Animal Spirit Guides* by Steven D. Farmer, Ph.D.).

Sturgis

For those of you not into the biker scene, there is a yearly bike rally in Sturgis, South Dakota that draws bikers from all around the country and all around the world. It is one of the largest bike rallies in the US and last year it drew over 500,000 people! Each year in August, bikers come to enjoy the beautiful Black Hills and spend time having fun and riding some of the best scenic roads in the US. When my friend asked me where I wanted to go for our bike trip after I retired, I immediately said STURGIS!

So, in August, we set off across this great country to ride to South Dakota. Fabulous does not even begin to describe this trip. To be able to see all of this great land from the road is so amazing. You can really feel the essence of the places you pass through. We live in such a beautiful place and it is so varied everywhere you go. From the North Carolina mountains whose twists and turns are born from an ancient mountain range, the Great Smokey mountains, we rode through Tennessee and saw and smelled some of the most beautiful green pastures. Then on through Kentucky, horse country! We saw the great horse farms along the road, each with their own unique estate name and emblem, and felt the age-old traditions of a place steeped in horse breeding and racing. Then on through Illinois and Missouri. We stopped in a small town along the Mississippi River to soak in the majesty of that roaring water. We stood beside the banks, listening to the sound of the flowing river and dreamed of Tom Sawyer and Huck Finn and all of the life adventures they had along the same river banks. If you close your eyes and listen in stillness, you can still hear them laughing. (*The Adventures of Tom Sawyer* by Mark Twain; *The Adventures of Huckleberry Finn* by Mark Twain).

Then on to the great city of St. Louis, home of the arch, baseball and beer. The plains of Missouri and Kansas were ripe with crops of wheat and soy beans and you can smell them as you pass. But the most amazing crop we saw was miles and miles of sunflowers. Their bright yellow faces following the sun. Sunflowers follow the sun with their faces from east to west and then turn their gaze to the east at the end of the day to wait for the next sunrise. Fabulous.

Through Kansas and on to Nebraska you see the cattle country. Miles and miles of grazing pasture land for the cattle. In the heat, you could see them trying to hide under a single tree to keep out of the sun, or wade in a small stream if one was available. And when they are loaded into a transport truck, you can hear them mooing at all different pitches to express what they are feeling at the time. And then finally into South Dakota. The Black Hills begin to rise up out of the plains and form the most mystic and colorful painting you could ever hope to see. And to be able to feel the temperature change on your skin, feel the air on your arms turn from humid to dry, smell the pungent earth and the dusty plains and feel the sun on your face - it is the most awakening feeling I think I have ever had.

When we were in South Dakota and we were riding one afternoon, we turned a corner to find that traffic had completely stopped. We stopped as well, and ahead of us was the most amazing sight you will ever see. There was a herd of buffalo coming straight at us! There were buffalo everywhere, to the right, to the left and in the middle of the road, coming straight toward us. As we sat on the bikes in utter amazement, a giant bull buffalo was heading our way. There was a cow with a calf right in front of him and he seemed to be anxious that they were not moving fast enough, so he was grunting and huffing at them as well as poking the cow with his mighty horns. It was the largest animal I have ever seen face to face! He must have weighed 2,000 pounds! His face was as long and large as his entire body and his black tongue was hanging out of his mouth. His coat was shaggy and dusty and it swayed with each step he took. As we sat completely frozen on the bikes, I began to become fearful of how close this mighty animal was to us and I think if I reached out, I could have touched him. I guess I stopped breathing for a few moments as I wondered whether he would decide we were in the wrong place at the wrong time and come straight toward us on the bikes. As he came even closer, I was also starting to wonder if we would survive a direct hit from this crazy bull. But just as he reached our bikes, he veered off to the left with the others and they continued on their way. It was clear that we were in their space but they were not out to harm anyone as long as we respected who they were. And we certainly did! To this day, it was the most fabulous animal encounter I have ever had.

The motorcycle rally itself is always fun and entertaining but the best part of the Sturgis Rally is the bike rides. Keystone and Mount Rushmore, Crazy Horse, Deadwood, Needles Highway, Badlands National Park and if you venture just over to the border to Wyoming, you can see Devil's Tower. These are some of the most mystical and magical places I have ever been and the connection with Mother Earth, indigenous tribes and all of the animals and nature will transform you into a different person by the time you leave. I don't think I have ever felt so connected to something greater and that feeling has never left me.

FABULOUS

FABULOUS

The Awakening

When I returned from the magical trip to Sturgis, I reached out to my "soulmate" to see about the pay back for the loan. I knew the relationship was over at this point and now I was just concentrating on getting the loan payments started. I texted him several times and there was always a reason why the money wasn't available yet. My ego kicked into overdrive and I began to believe that I had really gotten scammed. I remembered a part of the astrology reading that I had done the year before and found a very disturbing part:

"It is absolutely essential for you not to deceive yourself when it comes to love, romance and the true nature of other people. You can be incredibly naïve and easily seduced. Confusion, disappointments and regrettable mistakes in both emotional and financial matters may result." (www.compatible-astrology.com)

Wow. I convinced myself that he was a con man and had only ever seen me to scam money. I was beyond angry, hurt and embarrassed. I was on the phone one night with my best friend talking about what I should do next and she happened to look him up on Facebook. And that's where we found that he had been dating someone else since December of the prior year! In my mind, that solidified all of the thoughts my ego had conjured up and I was inconsolable. I sank into another depression. But this time I also wanted revenge. I went on the hunt for a lawyer so I could sue him for whatever I could get back. But none of the lawyers I reached out to would return my call. I looked into small claims court but the amount he owed me was larger than what they would settle in small claims. I took out my hatred and revenge on him through some nasty texts. It was so vile and hateful but I was so angry and hurt, I could not think what else to do. Of course, he responded in kind – you get back what you put out there. But in my gut, I was having second thoughts about the lawsuit and the hatred and the revenge. And so, I texted back that I could not believe our relationship had come to this and I was just seeking an apology to move on with my life.

And then I got a Note from the Universe:

> "It's always better to give too much, pay too much, and love too much, than not enough.
>
> But then, Anne, since everything comes back to you exponentially, can there ever be too much?
>
> I love you too much anyway,
> The Universe"
>
> ©www.tut.com

Thanks Mike Dooley (www.tut.com)! That's exactly what I needed to hear. And like everything since then, the timing of that exact message was no coincidence. It was instead a sign. I had always given from my heart and I had forgotten that somewhere along the way. There was also a note in one of the emails from The Universe about a book called *The Wisdom of the Council* by Sara Landon. I was drawn to that for an unknown reason and ordered it immediately. When I began to read that book, my life changed forever. I remembered who I was, why I was here and that we are all light beings on a great adventure here on earth. I realized that the religious beliefs I had been taught growing up were not the full truth and that I was a spirit being in a human body who was loved so immensely by Universal Consciousness that I could not go back to the density I had been living in for the past months. And at that one moment in time, all of the hatred, revenge, selfishness, regret, jealousy and shame just disappeared. **Literally, it was just gone**. And I felt a calm, loving feeling replace all of those negative emotions. I forgave my soulmate unconditionally in that moment and I forgave myself as well.

If you remember, I said that I was the kind of person that has to have an even scale when it comes to give and take and if that scale is not even, I can hold a grudge for a lifetime. Yet, that all disappeared as well. *Forever.* I kept waiting for it to come back, thinking I was just caught up in this book and eventually I would come back to my senses. But when you have an awakening like that, I find that there is no going back. Once you start awakening spiritually, you are in for eternity. And I could not be happier about it.

I told him all was forgiven and that I would always cherish our time together. He was my soulmate for a short time, truly. But the other thing I am learning is that you can have more than one soulmate in your life here on earth and beyond. It supports where you are on your journey and how you move forward. And it is OK.

Fast Forward Six Months

As I enter into six months of my awakening journey, every day is more and more fabulous. My entire perspective on who I am and what the world really is has changed intensely and permanently. And in fact, I have a hard time remembering what it was like to not be like this.

So, what changed me so drastically? It was remembering, starting down the path of becoming awakened. Remembering that we are all light beings and have been since the start. That we have lived thousands of lifetimes as these light beings, maybe here on Earth and maybe in other parts of the galaxies. That we chose to have an adventure on earth to discover new things, feel new feelings, learn truths about ourselves, experience the separation from All That Is, Universal Consciousness, The Great Spirit, God; and then remember that we are not and could not ever be separate from the love that is Universal Consciousness, the quantum field. We are all energy that just changes form, as is everything in our

Universe. And right now, we have chosen that form to be these incredibly sophisticated human bodies. And yes, these bodies will ultimately die, but that energy and spirit will not and cannot ever die and we will move on to new adventures.

When you look at your life from that perspective, as a light being, observing itself in human form, then you can begin to see that life, as we know it now, is really just a fabulous opportunity to play, learn and grow. Knowing that each one of us is part of the Divine and we chose to be here to first experience separation from the Universal Consciousness only to then remember our oneness again. How can you be sad, angry, hateful, jealous or any of those other dense emotions when you know that there is really only the most incredible love for you. This is all just meant to be a fun, learning adventure in eternity. How can you not savor every delicious morsel the Universe has to offer? The only real Hell is not remembering who you really are, a divine spirit in human form. And when you do finally remember, Heaven is already here on earth, every day, everywhere and in everyone. There is no power judging you or keeping a scorecard. There is no judgement other than what you impose on yourself. The one constant through it all is that consciousness and energy is everything and that there is really only love. A love so strong that it permeates every cell, every molecule, every atom of everything here on earth and beyond. And because of that consciousness and energy, you can and should have anything you want that supports the highest purpose for you and humankind. Because you can manifest that energy into anything you want. You do it every day now, whether you realize it or not.

Can you see the divinity in everything? Every person, every animal, every tree, every blade of grass, every rock, every moment. It's there – open your heart to it, feel it embrace you, receive the love it has to offer you and return that love for all others and all things. You can only do that through your heart, not your head. If each of us does this, our world will change in ways we cannot even imagine.

I spend my days now dedicating the mornings to meditation, visualization, yoga and music. The **music** playlist now consists of songs from Jason Mraz, Andy Grammer, Dan Fogelberg, Styx and Eddie Money. I offer for you to put on your headphones and listen to "Peace in Our Time" by Eddie Money or "Nether Lands" by Dan Fogelberg. I dare you not to smile and sing along.

The **animals** have also changed. I do spirit walks with animals most days and it is amazing which animal spirit shows up with just the right message I need at that time. (There is a great guided meditation journey to connect to animal spirits in the book *Animal Spirit Guides* by Steven D. Farmer, Ph.D.). The deer don't come like they used to even though they are still around. In one of my animal spirit walks, I called to the deer spirit to ask why I didn't see them anymore. The spirit said that I no longer needed them and they were out helping others now. I agreed and thanked them for their years of love and support. Now I enjoy spending time outside with the birds, the squirrels, the rabbits, the turtles and all the other critters and I find immense peace in just being around them. And mama deer did bring her new little one again this Spring. But this time she picked the herb garden next to my house, right under the blackberry bush to keep the new fawn safe. Precious.

I also use Tarot cards every morning. As I draw the card for the day, I ask Universal Consciousness to show me the message I need for the day and trust my "gut" intuition to guide me. My intuition is strongest as a gut feeling or clairsentience. So the use of Tarot cards helps me *feel* the connection to higher power, rather than seeing it or hearing it. And the guidance is absolutely remarkable.

I have looked at all sorts of other paths and continue to explore the ones that I feel a connection with. I have a strong connection to my guardian angel – his name is Ezrael. I feel him at my right shoulder and he is always there – always. If you don't know your guardian angel, be quiet, close your eyes and ask them to come to you. They will, because they want to have a relationship with you. But you have to ask them into your life. Do that. I also love learning about the Native Americans and their unique connection to the Great Spirit. The animal spirit walks come from that tradition.

I still love and cherish my **friends** as I always will. And I open the way for new friends who are experiencing their own awakening. I am finding that it seems everyone has their own definition of what awakening and transformation means. And that's OK. Just having people to talk to and ask questions of is reassuring as well as educational. And I so love my family. Most of my days are spent taking care of my amazing parents and it is a gift that I would never have thought could be so rewarding and so full of love. Learning who your parents are is a gift that doesn't come to everyone, and I am blessed to be able to receive that gift.

I have unconsciously migrated to a plant-based diet and feel the rewards of that every day. And I thank Mother Earth for all of her bounty each time I sit down to eat. I live in happiness most of the time, while still learning my lessons from the past and dealing with those emotions so that I can ultimately release the things that no longer serve me. And yes, I still deal with those wrinkles in my face! But some days I just cry tears of joy for absolutely no reason other than the beauty in our world.

I know there are a lot of books and seminars on positive thinking and how great it is for you and how it can support you in achieving whatever you want. And I totally believe that it is all true and it is how you manifest happiness, wealth, health and relationships. I use and practice it every day. But when you can add remembering your connection to Universal Consciousness, it pales in comparison. You will go from manifesting material things to manifesting happiness and joy, knowing that everything will flow from that. When you can feel the deepest joy you have ever known, feel the deepest love you can have in your heart, feel unconditional love for yourself and everyone else, you will know a new kind of happiness that you can experience EVERY day of your life here on earth. That's what my definition of what becoming awakened means.

Fast Forward Six Months

Turn off your phone
Sit in nature and be still
Smell the fragrance of a beautiful flower
Listen to the music of the birds
Hug a tree
Enjoy the bounties of the gracious mother earth
Love your family and friends
Do some yoga
Meditate
Sing to the top of your lungs
Imagine
Receive
Breathe

Love yourself for who and what you are right now, in this moment, and get lost in the joy that is yours to have.

And never, *ever* forget how immensely loved you really are.

And so it is.

And it is FABULOUS.

FABULOUS

Your Homework

OK, so no one really likes homework I guess but make this a fun thing! **For just one day**, notice yourself through the day and what you are thinking about yourself, what you are thinking about others and what you are saying. For this one day, be like an outside observer of yourself – no judgement – just awareness.

Make note of the things you say to yourself when you look in the mirror; make note of the things you think about when you are driving, make note of the things you say when someone does something you don't agree with or looks like someone you don't relate to; make note of the things you say when you are shopping or paying your bills. And notice the last thoughts you have before you go to sleep.

Awareness is one of the key paths to knowing yourself and that's what this is all about. Ask yourself how you would feel if you knew someone was saying those things about you. Are your thoughts loving to yourself and others? When you notice you are feeling angry or hurt, are you accepting those feelings and looking at why or are you ignoring and perhaps repressing those feelings?

Now, do you like that person that you noticed for a day? Would that person be someone you would want to spend time with?

We all grow and change every minute and awareness of how that change is impacting your thoughts and words is the first step to becoming you as your best self. Make every thought and every word reflect the wonderful person that you are. And although it's not always easy, it is always rewarding.

www.ingramcontent.com/pod-product-compliance
Lightning Source LLC
Chambersburg PA
CBHW061749070526
44585CB00025B/2846